Motorbike

© The Archon Press Ltd 1976

First published in Great Britain
by Hamish Hamilton
Children's Books Ltd
90 Great Russell Street
London WC1B 3PT

0 241 89525 1

Printed in Great Britain by
W. S. Cowell Ltd
Butter Market, Ipswich

Reprinted 1976

Originated by David Cook and
Associates and produced by
The Archon Press Ltd,
28 Percy Street, London W1P 9FF

Acknowledgements

Author: Mike Bygrave   Art Director: Jim Bulman
Special Consultant: Jim Dowdall   Designer: Malcolm Smythe

Illustration sources: Where more than one artist or photographer contributed
the illustrations to a spread, these are listed from A to Z, starting with the
picture farthest to the left and nearest the top of the page and working
down each column in turn.

Cover Colour, Roy Coombs:
       logo, Mike Reid

2–3   National Motor Museum
4–5   John Davies
6–7   A: *Motor Cycle*: B,C:
       Vic Barnes: D: Malcolm
       Smythe
8–9   A: Roy Coombs: B,C: Tom
       Brittain
10–11 A: Trevor Hill/Venner
       Studios: B,C,D,E,F: Keith
       Harmer
12–13 A: Tom Brittain: B,C,D,E,F:
       Jim Bulman: G,H,I: *Motor
       Cycle*
14–15 A,B: Science Museum:
       C,D: The Olyslager
       Organisation: E: Roy
       Coombs: F,G: National
       Motor Museum
16–17 A,C,D: David Palmer: B:
       Science Museum: E:
       National Motor Museum:
       F: *Motor Cycle*
18–19 A: Jim Dowdall: B: Terry
       Collins: C,E: B. H. Vander-
       veen: D: Vic Barnes
20–1   A,B,F: Malcolm Smythe:

       C: *Motor Cycle*: D: Nick
       Nicholls: E: Popperfoto
22–3   A,E: Vic Barnes: B,D: Nick
       Nicholls: C: Bill Hamilton/
       Camera Press
24–5   A,B,D,E: Nick Nicholls: C:
       Tom Brittain
26–7   David Strickland
28–9   A,B: Mike Patrick: C,D:
       Tom Brittain: E: Nick Nicholls
30–1   A,B,E: Roger Gorringe: C:
       Yamaha (UK) Ltd: D: Roy
       Coombs
32–3   A,C,D,E,H: Jan Heese:
       B,F: Malcolm Smythe:
       G: F. W. Reynolds
34–5   A,C,D,E,F,G: Jan Heese:
       B,H: Malcolm Smythe
36–7   A,B,C: David Strickland:
       D: Malcolm Smythe
38–9   A: David Strickland: B,C:
       Jan Heese: D: Terry Collins:
       E: Vic Barnes
40–1   A,B,C: David Strickland:
       D: Rickman Brothers: E:
       E. T. Budge
42–3   A: Phil Mather: B: Tom
       Brittain: C,E: Fred Enke:
       D: Mick Woollett
44–5   David Strickland

and special thanks to:

Viv Croot for editorial research; Tony Reed at the Olyslager Organisation;
Dave Mackinson for his collection of Vincents; Ray, the Ossa owner
(pp. 26/7), and his mate; Dave Minton; the staffs of *Motor Cycle, Motor
Cycle News, Motor Cycle Weekly*; E. T. Budge & Associates; Norton Villiers
at Wolverhampton; Maggi Loan for her great help; Michael McGuinness for
the instant graphics and Lynette Trotter for picture research.

Motor Bike

HAMISH HAMILTON · LONDON

Motorcycle World

Bikes are much more than just a vaguely uncomfortable form of transport: they're a way of life. Riding a motorbike is a physical pleasure, one of the few left open in this mass-produced, centrally-heated age. The wind in your hair, the throb of the motor beneath you, seemingly unlimited power at your hand (not at your foot, as in a car), your body reflecting every little nuance of the bike's performance, *feeling* the road as you flash above it. . . . People who ride motorbikes tend to love machines for their own sakes. The motorbike was one of the last great machines invented before technology became a matter of flashing lights and electronic brains. You can *see* how a bike works and you don't need a degree in nuclear physics to repair one. Most bikers are their own mechanics, and you'll find them spending as much time lying under their machines in greasy overalls as they do straddling them in immaculate leathers.

The biker's world is a basic one, and that's where we start too. We take you step by step through the construction of a modern motorbike, with a few backward glances at the way the old boneshakers of yesteryear were put together. Then we look at the history of the bike, a short and glorious one, spanning about eighty years, from the end of the last century, and taking in two world wars when bikes, some fitted with machine guns, became deadly weapons. To leap from warfare to a modern motorcycle road race may seem a big jump, but the BMWs that dominate the sidecar classes today are substantially the same bikes used by the German Army.

Modern motorbike racing has excitement and glamour and its own set of heroes, from youthful, dashing Barry Sheene, who has fallen off a motorbike at 170 mph and lived, to mature, wily competitors like Italy's Giacomo Agostini and Britain's Phil Read. Then it's across to the freezing moorlands of the north of England or the winter backwoods of America for some different kinds of racing that any biker can enjoy – scrambling, hill climbs, trials riding or, in summer,

grass-track or drag. A modern motorcycle is a performance machine, and the urge to squeeze that little bit more power, that extra edge of speed out of your steed is a strong one.

Modern motorbikes come in a bewildering array of shapes and sizes. We take you through the card, from the tiny Honda 50 ccs (don't knock them – they laid the foundation of the mighty Japanese motorcycle industry), through the 175s and 250s – probably the most common size on the road today – to the classic 500, and upwards into the 'superbike' range, where a motorcycle becomes a piece of precision machinery like a watch. Then there are The Giants, built for luxury touring, not speed, these machines really behave!

Finally, a detailed look at some of motorcycling's myths with choppers and café racers. Are they motorbikes or extensions of their owner's private fantasies? What sort of people build and ride them? And why? Whatever the answers, they're a tiny minority of riders as our last spread shows. Here we interview three typical, but very different bikers.

But this book is dedicated to all bikers – from chopper freaks to Sunday scramblers – who put in all their skill and spare time in order to experience the sense of freedom and mastery that only a bike can give!

Basic Bikes

A modern motorcycle is not just a bicycle with an engine mounted on it. It's a totally different machine. Early motorbikes ran on steam. The very first motorbikes, created in the 1870s and 1880s, were simply adapted bicycles, and the early inventors could never decide where to put the engine – they tried it in front of the handlebars; above the rear wheel and below the saddle; and, in more than one design, it appeared behind and virtually detached from the bike itself, like a trailing bomb. By the early 1890s, designers had switched from steam to the internal combustion engine and settled on an engine position low down between the wheels – thus ensuring a reasonable distribution of weight and lowering the height of the bike's centre of gravity. (It was now much more difficult to fall off a motorbike.) The engine also became an integral part of the frame of the bike, instead of a mere appendage. The new machine was practical, controllable and, essentially, a modern motorbike.

The basic design of the motorbike has changed surprisingly little since then. In common with a bicycle, it has two wheels, handlebars, a saddle and, often, a chain drive. But features like the suspension (lacking in the early 'bone-shakers' – aptly named), braking systems, gearing, frame construction, improved tyres and, of course, the motor itself make the motorcycle of the 1970s a very different animal.

The bike starts here – this cradle frame, the standard modern type, is made of an amalgam of tubular and pressed-steel. Note steering yoke at front, engine mount, saddle and tank mounts.

After being stove enamelled, the frame is ready to receive the 500 cc twin-cylinder, air-cooled, 4-stroke Honda engine. Engine and gearbox are contained in the single unit construction. Also added at this stage are swinging arm rear suspension, and front teledraulic forks.

The bike takes on a recognisable shape with the addition of the spoked wheels, petrol tank, exhaust pipes and brakes (drum type on the rear wheel and disc on the front). The completed machine (**right**) sports full electrics, handlebars, instrumentation, mirrors, saddle, mudguards and paint.

The front disc brake is connected up to hydraulics in the handlebars. Bike has optional kick/electric start.

Over 50 years separate the 1917 Triumph Model H and the 1975 Honda CB500 Twin, and despite a very similar engine capacity, the bikes look and handle very differently. The Honda is a typical 70s streetbike, built for stability, comfort and easy cruising in the mid-speed range, and complete with sophisticated electric and exhaust systems. The Model H, a far more rugged proposition, was a light, easily manoeuvrable machine. Although the top speed was only 50 mph, the bike was extremely powerful at low revs, which made it very useful in the mud-fields of Flanders. The simple systems were easily repaired by the rider.

A comparison between Triumph Model 'H' of 1917 and the Honda CB500 Twin of 1975		
	Triumph	**Honda**
ENGINE CONFIGURATION	Single cylinder	Twin cylinder in parallel
	Side valve	Double Overhead Camshaft
	4 stroke	4 stroke
	85 mm × 88 mm bore	70 mm × 64·8 mm bore
ENGINE CAPACITY	550 cc	498 cc
GEARS	3 speed	5 speed
FUEL CONSUMPTION	80 mpg 26·5 km/l	70 mpg 24 km/l
TOP SPEED	50 mph 80·5 kph	105 mph 168·95 kph
DRIVE	Primary by chain	Chain throughout
	Final by belt	
KERB WEIGHT	250–300 lbs 113–136 kg	426 lbs 193 kg
FUEL TANK CAPACITY	1·5 gallons 6·821 litres	3·5 gallons 15·921 litres

Like most early bikes, the Triumph catered for rough riders with no rear suspension and a bicycle-type saddle. Horses were kinder.

Known as 'The Trusty' because of its reliability, the 1917 Triumph was a British Army mainstay for dispatch work in the First World War. Still more motor-assisted-cycle than modern motorbike, the Triumph had a single-cylinder engine with side-valves, a chain-driven magneto for ignition, 3-speed gears and a hand-operated oil pump. Braking is by block-and-pulley rear brake and bicycle brake at front.

The front lamp was a carbide while the rear light (not shown) gave less light than a candle.

Clearly shown as the 'wheel within a wheel' is the Triumph's belt-drive, soon to be abandoned in favour of the chain.

The Honda CB500 is typical of the middle-range of modern motorcycles. Oil lubrication and the advance-and-retard, both hand-operated on the Triumph, have become automatic. The foot-operated gears allow 5 speeds and there is an electric starter. Comfort — meaning suspension — has improved out of recognition with teledraulics (front) and the swinging arm system (rear), as has engine performance.

The Honda's double saddle — the Triumph was single-seat — lifts up to show a tool kit and fuse box. Note also the 3·5 gallon tank with quick-release cap.

Like many modern bikes, Honda select fast-action disc brakes for the front wheels and the more gradual drum for the rear, giving the rider more feel and cutting down the danger of locking the rear wheel.

The Engine

The internal combustion engine is the object under the bonnet of a car which causes 99 per cent of drivers to panic every time it goes wrong. People who would leap to repair a burst pipe or put up a shelf, turn pale at the sight of a spark plug. Bikers are a tougher breed. Perhaps because they can actually see their engines, they have learned to live with them and often love them as a thing of beauty and a toy forever. Bikers are mostly enthusiastic amateur mechanics. There are more magazines for bikers, telling them how to do everything from change a tyre to rebuild a bike, than there are for any other group of people, except possibly gardeners.

The principle of the internal combustion engine is pretty simple. A piston moves up and down in a cylinder, propelled by small explosions from above of an air-and-petrol mixture. (This is the 'internal combustion' of the title, since it all takes place inside the cylinder.) This up and down movement is converted into a rotary motion by the crankshaft. A belt, chain or shaft transmits the rotary motion to the wheels and can be interrupted along its length by a set of gears. Meanwhile, the carburettor mixes the petrol and air and the spark plugs do what they sound like – provide the spark which ignites the internal explosions.

Torque is a twisting force tending to cause motion. Bikers call good bikes 'nice and torquey' but find it hard to explain what this is. Our diagram shows you.

So far, so good. But what makes one engine different from or better than another?

Engines differ in size, for one thing, and this is expressed in cubic capacity – the area covered by the sweep of the piston. In other words, roughly the size of the cylinder. Engines have different numbers of cylinders, too, although more of them doesn't necessarily mean more speed. Basically, the more cylinders, the more 'torque' you get – a twisting force which causes rotation. Think of a spinning bicycle wheel: torque is the amount of pressure you'd have to

This cutaway of a Honda 500 cc engine shows (1) the camshaft, operated by a drive chain (2) with a tension adjuster (3). (4) is the high point of the cam itself, (5) the rocker for the operating valve and (6) leads to the rev counter. The driving sprocket for the cam chain (7) is on the crankshaft. (8) is just an idler sprocket for the cam chain. That completes the overhead camshaft mechanism, whose purpose is to open and close the valves (9) on the head of the piston (10) while the spark plug (11) ignites the petrol and air mixture fed in by the carburettor (18). (12) is the clutch, (13) the gears, (14) the kickstart gear, (15) the gearbox sprocket and (16) the final drive chain to the rear wheel sprocket (17). (The diagram shows two cams but only one piston/carburettor, for clarity.)

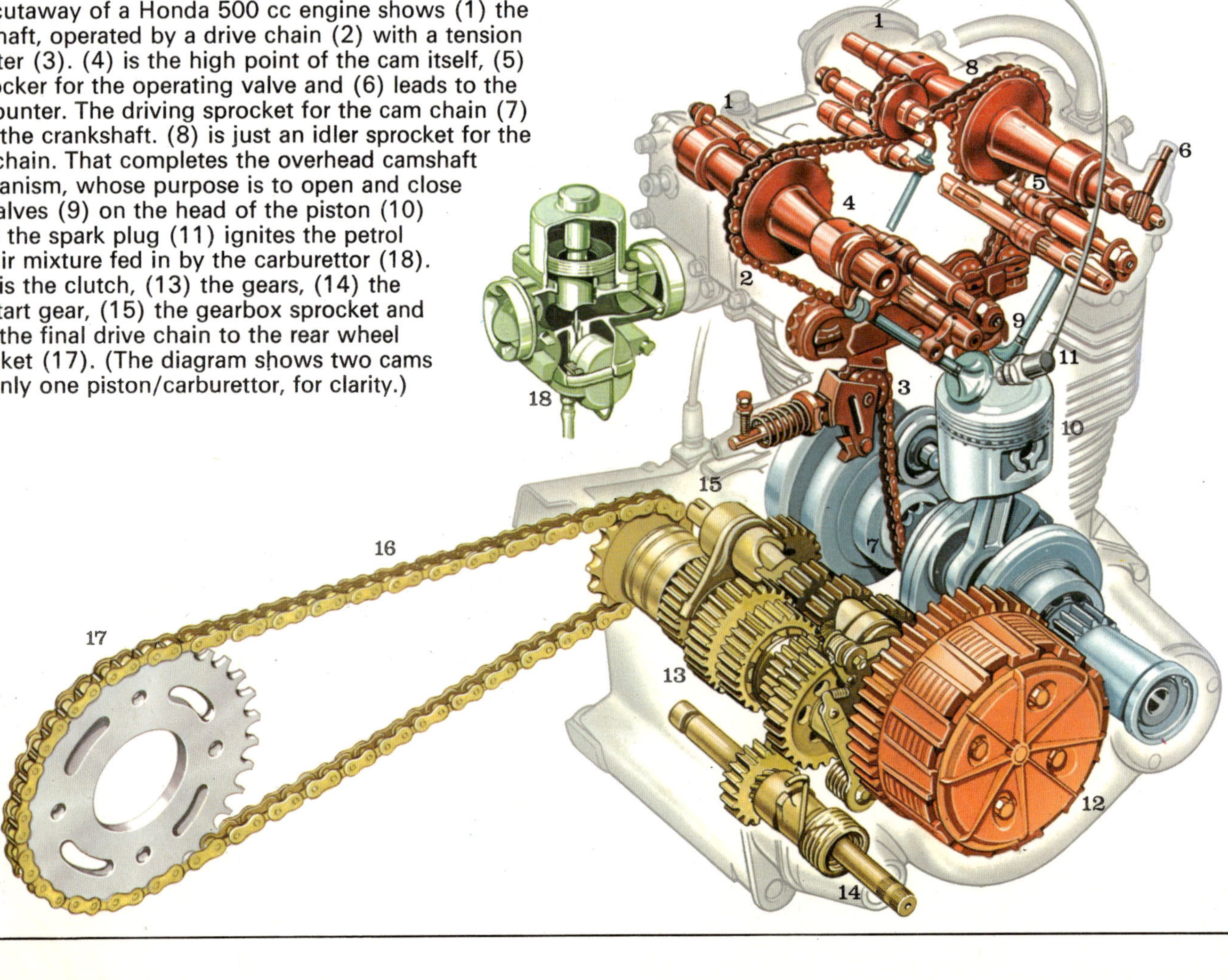

The piston/crankcase complex: the piston, operating inside the cylinder, is forced into a falling motion by an explosion in the cylinder head – caused by the ignition of the petroleum and air mixture (via an electric current). The crankshaft is turned by the eccentrically located connecting rod. The rotation of the crankshaft then moves the gears and, finally, the wheels.

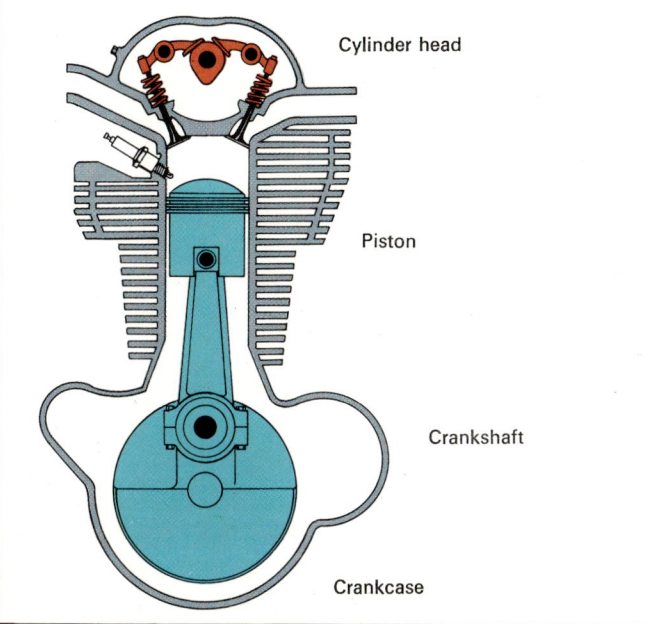

Cylinder head

Piston

Crankshaft

Crankcase

exert to stop it. The result is a more flexible machine with better performance all round. American bikes were mainly twin-cylinders from the start – to ride long distances at high speeds on straight roads. European single-cylinder machines avoided the weight and vibration problems of multi-cylinder bikes (and they saved on petrol!).

Engines differ between two-stroke and four-stroke. Again, this doesn't necessarily affect their speed, nor does it have anything to do with the number of cylinders they have. A two-stroke engine works on a slightly different principle from a four-stroke. The piston takes only two strokes to complete each cycle instead of four, and there are no valves to let in the mixture and expel the exhaust gases. Two-strokes are easier to manufacture and maintain. They also tend to have faster acceleration and a better balanced centre of gravity (which accounts for two-stroke dominance in scrambling). On the other hand, when you stop a two-stroke, you're relying entirely on your brakes. With a four-stroke, as you change down through the gears, the engine itself helps to slow you down (virtually all cars are four-stroke).

Engines also differ between long-stroke and short-stroke. Long-stroke engines have less acceleration but last longer and are especially good for long-distance performances. They have a lot of power at low speeds. Most long strokes are 'twins' or 'singles', but the famous vintage American bikes, the Henderson 'fours' (four-cylinder) were long-strokes.

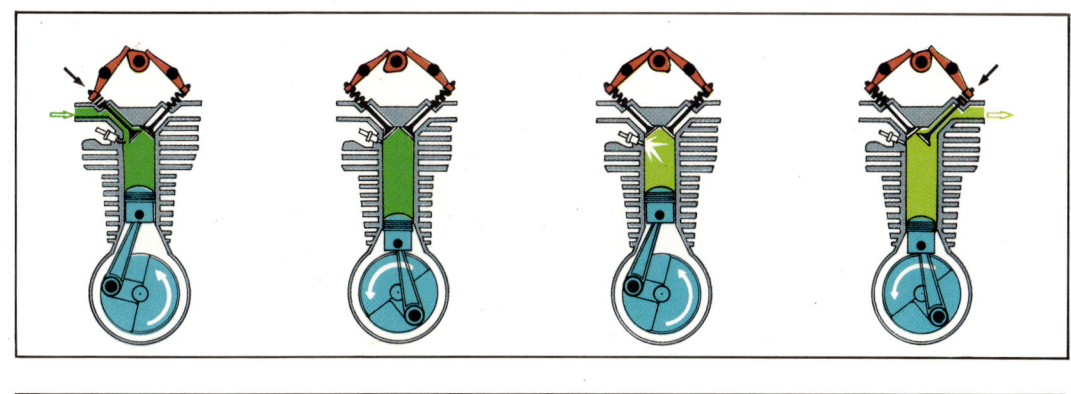

Four-stroke engines.
First stroke (*far left*) is induction stroke: piston lowers, cam opens inlet valve, petrol and air are sucked into cylinder. In the compression stroke: inlet valve closes and piston raises, compressing petrol and air. Power stroke: spark plug ignites mixture.
Fourth (*right*), the exhaust stroke.

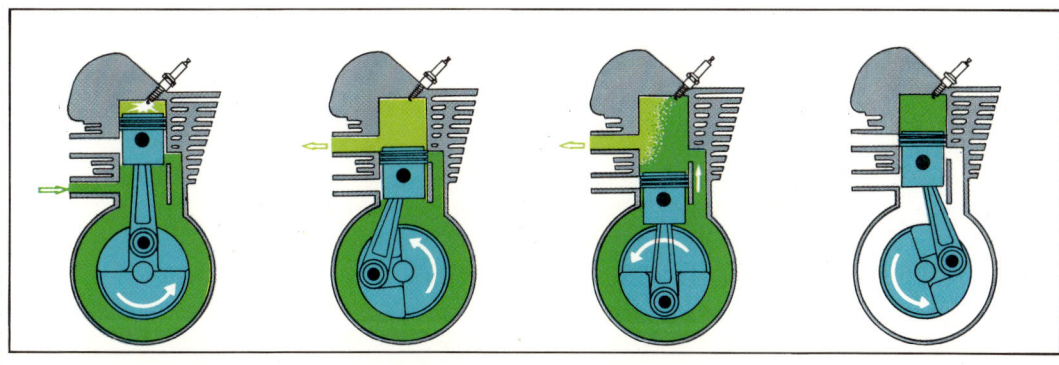

Two-stroke engines.
First stroke (*far left*) compresses fuel already in cylinder, draws new fuel into crankcase. Second stroke is power stroke. Other two diagrams show how lowering piston opens exhaust inlet, spent gases escape, transfer port inside cylinder then opens, allowing compressed crankcase fuel to spurt up into cylinder.

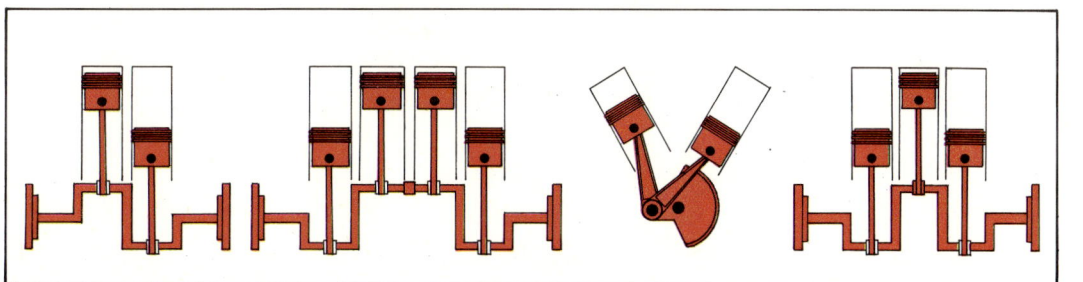

Cylinder arrangements.
There are numerous ways of arranging the cylinders in an engine, some of which have become company trademarks, like Harley Davidson's use of the V-twin. Bikes are often described by the number and arrangement of their cylinders.

Bike Systems

Go over any pothole in a car, and the worst you'll do is take a few days off its life. Go over a pothole on a motorbike and you'll know you've been in a fight. Bikes are sensitive machines: brakes, suspension, gears, transmission, tyres can all make a big difference to how well a bike performs and to the length of its life.

Early bikes were belt driven. When they stopped, the immortal cry went up from passers-by: 'The rubber band broke!' Chains were replacing belts by the early 1900s. As bikes have become more powerful, primary transmission (from the engine to the clutch) has been reinforced in some bikes by a second or even a third chain. Gears now play their part in primary transmission: old bikes had no gears, so transmission was direct from the engine to the belt and you couldn't change from one speed to another. The rule is, the more gears you have, the more flexibly your bike will perform. Modern bikes are mainly 5-speed; some are 6-speed.

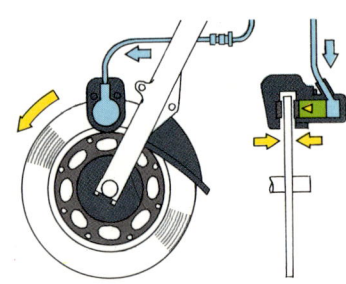

Disc Brakes (right): twin calipers, hydraulically operated from a master cylinder on the handlebars, pinch a central disc to give fast, positive braking. Self-adjusting but not so effective in the wet; drilled for lightness.

Drum Brakes (left): tension on a cable causes the two shoes to expand outwards via a camming motion. Fibre pads brake against drum interior. More gradual than disc braking; needs regular adjustment to maintain correct tension.

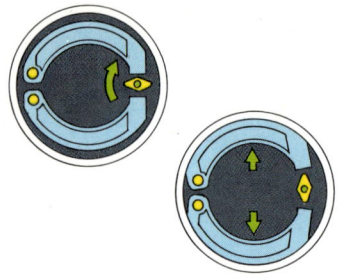

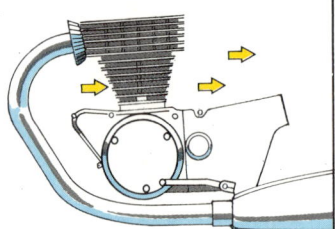

Air-cooling (right): the reason for those funny fins around a standard motorbike engine. Much thought goes into an aerodynamic design which will increase the air flow, especially to the rear of the engine.

Water-cooling (left): some modern bikes are water-cooled. Like a car radiator without the fan, it still adds weight.

Basic Suspension Systems

Front Shock Absorber (left): fixed lower section, filled with oil, absorbs the moving plunger. Spring in plunger returns it to its original position. This combination of telescope action and hydraulics is known as 'teledraulics' and is the standard design.

British police bikes used to be built with special gearing to give them faster acceleration – and lower top speeds.

In theory, shaft drive should have replaced the chain some time around the 1940s. It didn't happen and, with the exception of BMWs, which have been shaft-driven for years, the majority of modern bikes still rely on chains. One reason for this may be cheapness and ease of manufacture – there are minimal advantages to be gained from chains in terms of decreased weight and a (very small) increase in power; but shafts don't slip or break as easily as chains do. Secondary transmission (of power to the wheels) is still by chain on the majority of present-day bikes.

Modern motorcycle clutches are basically of two kinds: the diaphragm clutch, used on Nortons, Triumphs, BSAs and BMWs; and the multiple plate working in oil which is a feature of the Japanese bikes. There is little to choose between the two types from the point of view of efficiency.

Once you've got your bike going, it's important to be able

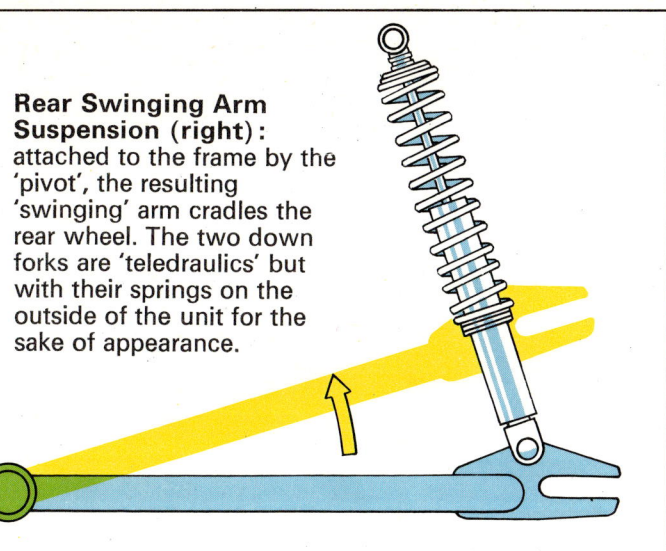

Rear Swinging Arm Suspension (right): attached to the frame by the 'pivot', the resulting 'swinging' arm cradles the rear wheel. The two down forks are 'teledraulics' but with their springs on the outside of the unit for the sake of appearance.

to stop it quickly and safely. It took the Japanese to make disc brakes a standard feature of modern motorbikes, in the early 1970s; which just shows how conservative the European motorcycle industry used to be. The technology of discs (which are hydraulically operated, like a car's brakes, and which have superior stopping power) was known. Manufacturers simply didn't bother to apply it, though disc brakes are cheaper to produce. Some modern machines have discs front and rear; but drum brakes on the rear wheel give more gradual and controllable braking.

Chain Drive (below): chains replaced belts as the driving mechanism for bikes during the early 1900s. Note that two chains are used.

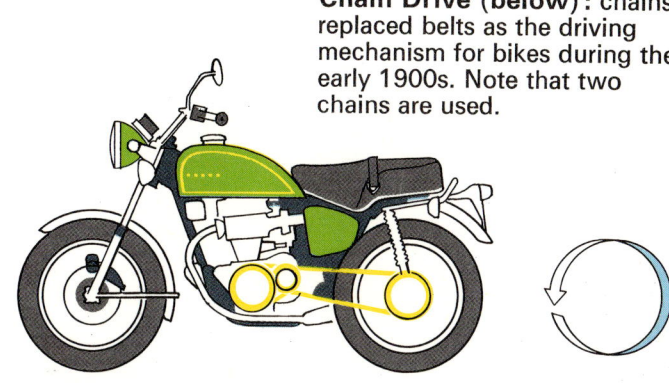

Shaft Drive (below): Shaft drive needs less maintenance and is more reliable than chain, but is heavier and more expensive to manufacture.

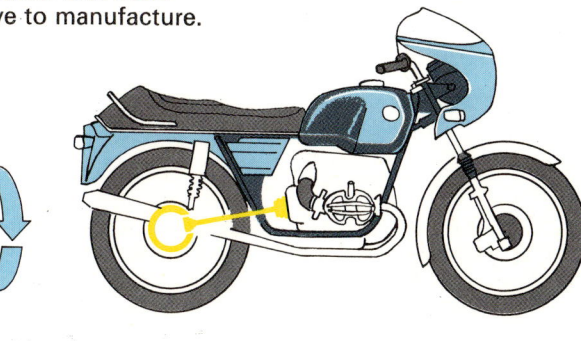

Tyres:

All Weather:
Motorcyle tyres in general tend to be treaded more around the walls than car tyres because bikes lean over to corner.

Scramblers:
You can always tell a scrambling bike by its distinctive knobbly tyres for greater traction.

Drag Slicks:
Extra-wide treadless tyres are spun very fast before races to make them sticky and improve adhesion. Rate of tyre development has determined the size of drag bikes.

Early Bikes

From the days when motorbikes were one of the most popular forms of family transport comes this early Triumph. The native servant was optional.

The first motorcycles, like the Michaux velocipede of 1868–9, ran on steam. They were ordinary pedal cycles, the 'bone-shakers' of the day, with small steam units attached to drive the back wheel by means of pulleys and a belt. But fitting a steam engine on a bicycle was like trying to ride while carrying the kitchen sink; and it was only when the internal combustion engine was developed (in Germany in 1876) that the motorbike became a practical proposition. With the development of the Werner motorcycle in France (1896), a simple, belt-driven machine, with an engine mounted on the steering head of the frame, a new era in motorcycling began.

From 1900, there were things called 'motorbikes' on two continents – Europe and America – and a rash of small engineering firms were turning them out: Indians, Excelsiors, Harley Davidsons in America; Zeniths, Scotts, Matchless, Belgian FNs in Europe. To look at now, those early bikes are like the skeletons of the modern machines, bare and bony but with a pleasing purity. They have thin, spindly frames, small petrol tanks, narrow, bicycle-type saddles and slender wheels. By 1914, America was beginning to take the lead in

Top left, the world's first petrol engine motorbike, built in Germany in 1885 by Gottlieb Daimler.

Centre, a bicycle with motor attached, this 1899 machine was built in Paris by the brothers Werner.

Bottom left, 1900, Britain's Singer company put the engine in the front wheel – and the family in danger.

The 1914 American Militaire looked as if it was made out of everything except the kitchen sink. It was only the second 4-cylinder bike made in the USA and its inventor thought of it as a 2-wheeled car. It was ahead of its time but production was stopped in 1922.

Jake de Rossier racing an American Indian machine at Brooklands in 1911. American firms led the world in producing bikes for racing purposes.

Sidecars could be quite elegant, as this Henderson combination shows. Hendersons were manufactured by Ignaz Schwinn, one of America's bike pioneers.

technical development which had originally been given by France and Germany.

In America, however, thanks to the genius of Henry Ford, who pioneered the assembly-line method of making cars, there was never a mass market for motorbikes as basic transport. But the Americans were keen to use bikes for sport.

In Britain, the Tourist Trophy Races on the Isle of Man had begun in 1907 and were to prove a valuable stimulus to technical development. For the first races, the limiting capacities of the bikes entered were 500 cc for single-cylinder machines and 750 cc for twin-cyclinders. The standardisation of machines based on engine cylinder capacity had originated on the Continent, where it was first used to

regulate entries in racing and hill climbs.

By 1914, the motorbike was well established and already had an aura of adventure, created by people like 'Cannonball' Baker who set out from California in 1914 to cross America. He rode an Indian V-twin and carried a revolver. A weather expert helped him to plan the route to avoid bad weather – which could make the dirt roads of the time impassable. He sent extra gasoline ahead of him by rail and had mules pack it from the stations to special caches in the wilds: there were no garages in the desert then. He fell off several times and had a lot of trouble with dogs. He shot three. After eleven days, twelve hours and ten minutes, he reached New York. Baker – and the motorcycle – had arrived.

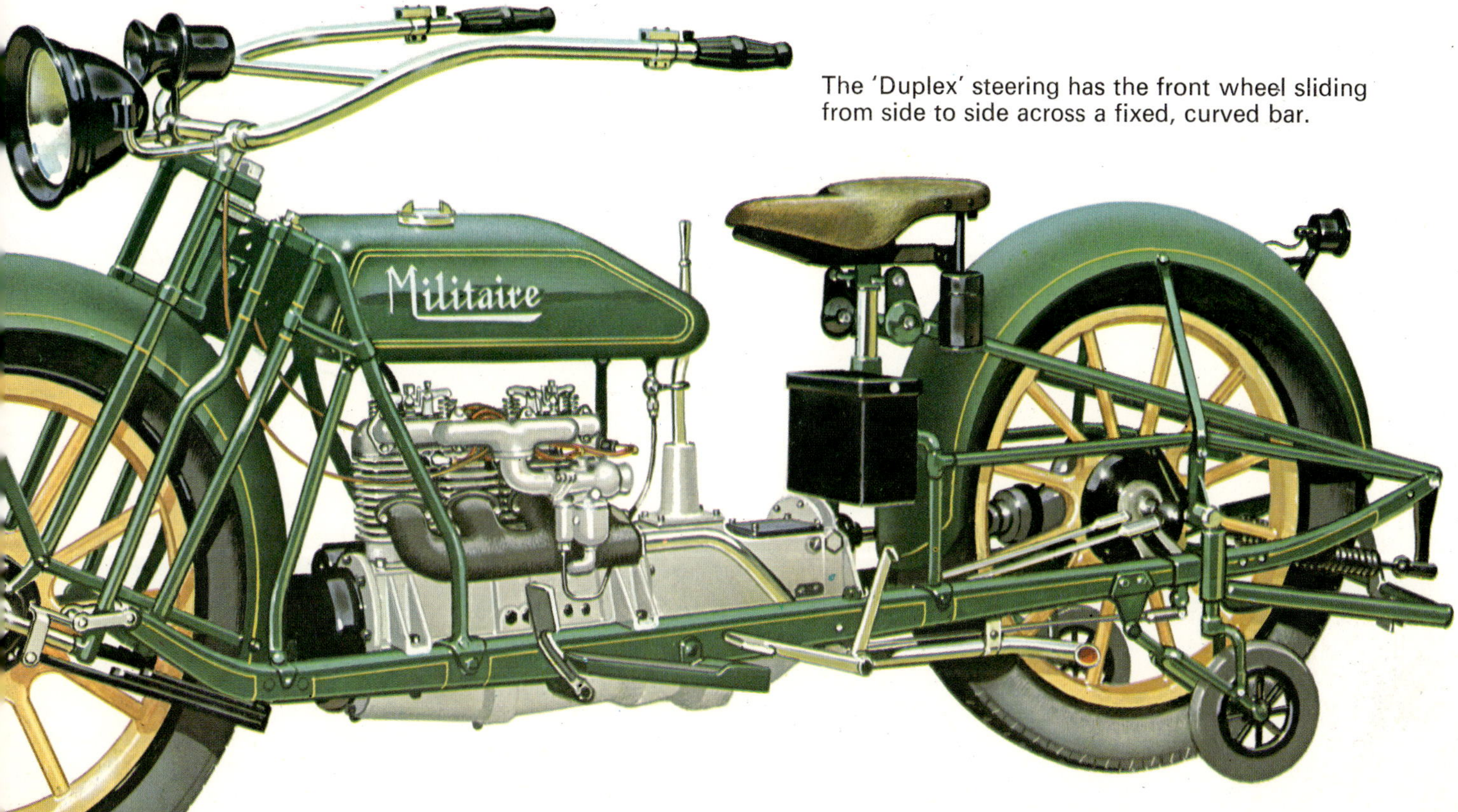

The 'Duplex' steering has the front wheel sliding from side to side across a fixed, curved bar.

The two sidewheels were supposed to act as stabilisers when the bike went slowly, and also as a stand.

The Twenties and Thirties

Billed as 'the fastest motorcycle in the world', the American Ace 4-cylinder bike was made from 1920 to 1926. The company backed its claim with record runs up to 129 mph.

The European motorbike developed rapidly in the 1920s and 1930s. By the mid-thirties it had entered its 'Golden Age', which was to last for twenty years. The most successful and reliable European bikes were British. They were single-cylinder, four-stroke machines. They were cheaper to manufacture and suited a country with winding roads, expensive petrol and a twenty-mile-an-hour speed limit.

Racing – always a good indication of the health of the bike industry – spread throughout Europe in the 1920s. Europeans preferred road racing, on ordinary roads closed to the public, to the American dirt-track or endurance runs. By 1930 there was a properly organised system of Grand Prix, with races in Belgium, Holland, Italy, Ulster and the Isle of Man (the famous TT races), with different classes for different sizes of bikes. British manufacturers, especially Norton and Velocette, won 'on the island' with monotonous regularity. The riders in these early Grand Prix faced special hazards:

This 1930 Husqvarna was Sweden's contribution to biking, 350 cc and 500 cc V-twins were successful in road racing at the time. Today, Husqvarna make mainly specialist bikes for scrambling and speedway.

there were few safety precautions and road surfaces were rough and pot-holed.

By 1930, the standard British single-cylinder machine was being challenged by the Germans and Italians with multi-cylinder engines. The Germans, in particular, decided to forget about handling and concentrate on power (although in those days there were unresolved engineering problems about fitting very powerful engines into a motorbike frame). By 1939, Germany was ready to dominate the motorcycling world. BMW and NSU had developed special racing bikes apart from their normal production models. By the 1930s, Germany was the biggest bike-producing nation.

Meanwhile, away from the tracks, every man could and did ride a motorbike. He probably bought it after reading in an advertisement that it had won one of the big races. He was able to afford it, at a time of economic depression, because mass production techniques kept prices down. Ask someone in the 1930s for his idea of a typical 'biker', and he'd describe a family man, perhaps a skilled worker, in a floppy 'aviator's'

Below, a 1922 'Beezer' (BSA) with sidecar was the working man's favourite transport in Britain between the wars. Its V-twin 985 cc engine cruised at 50 mph.

helmet and a long raincoat, his lunch slung over his shoulder in a canvas satchel and, on weekends, the wife and kids in a sidecar beside him. Sidecars (and pillion seats) developed in this period, as did weatherproofing generally, in competition with the comfort provided by the new 'baby' cars.

While bikes boomed in Europe, the motorcycle industry in America had been all but wiped out by the all-conquering car. Before they went under, American firms had a brief revival with their famous 'fours' – giant, four-cylinder machines. (They even spread to Europe, where FN made one.) But the 'four' had cooling problems, among other things, and the day of the really successful, multi-cylinder machine was thirty years away.

In 1931, Ignaz Schwinn, owner of the big Excelsior/Henderson works, gathered his closest aides about him. 'Boys,' he said, 'today we stop'. That left Harley Davidson and Indian as the last manufacturers in America, surviving on their sales to enthusiasts and – very important during the gangster era of Prohibition – their police contracts.

The 1929 Sunbeam team at the Isle of Man. They won the Senior TT that year, during the 'Golden Age' of British bike manufacturers.

Below, a 1935 German Zundapp 500 cc machine, featuring shaft drive, unit construction 2-cylinder engine with completely encased carburettor and car-type gear shift.

Above, 'the Rolls Royce of motorbikes' was Britain's 1930 Brough Superior. They were very fast for their day (over 100 mph). T. E. Lawrence ('Lawrence of Arabia') was killed on one.

Military Bikes

In 1914, and again in 1939, Europe went to war on motorbikes. In the First World War, bikes took over from horses. Motorcycles were faster and easier to pull out of the mud of the Western Front than a horse – and they didn't need so much looking after. The British Army led with the use of bikes for dispatch work in 1914–18. Casualties were high, and a few days' tuition at home was not adequate preparation for the giant scrambling course that was the Somme and Ypres.

The latest despatch
"SEND MORE MEN!"
from the Sportsman's Battalions

Douglas

Age 19 to 45
Head Recruiting Office
HOTEL CECIL, LONDON

P. C. BURTON & C? L?? LONDON. W.C.

MILITARY POLICE

A 45-cubic inch Harley Davidson was a big beast, even in civilian life. Rigged out in fighting mood, with the special holder for a sub-machine gun, the 45WLA's were supplied in their thousands to the American, British and Canadian armies in World War Two, where they were mainly used for communications and staff work – or the Military Police!

Right, the Moto Guzzi D, 500 cc, was the Italian version of the German blitzkrieg bikes. Note the front-mounted machine gun and the 'sprung' frame – an elaborate design of hinged rear suspension which gives the bike its set-back look.

The most widely used makes in the British ranks were Douglas and Triumph. When the Americans came into the war, they brought over Harley Davidsons, Hendee/Indians and Clevelands.

By 1939, armies were thoroughly mechanised. This time, it was the German Army, which had relied on horses in 1914–18, which took the lead. Very large numbers of motorcycles (mainly DKWs) were employed by the Wehrmacht between 1939 and 1945. Many of their mechanised infantry divisions consisted of motorcyclists, used as part of the 'Blitzkrieg' strategy of lightning, attacking warfare, and they provided a classic example of the military use of two-wheeled vehicles. In 1937, BMW had designed the 750 cc R75, an astonishingly modern bike, years ahead of its time, with a reverse gear, four-speed gearbox, shaft drive, hydraulic brakes, telescopic front forks and a revolutionary shaft drive to the sidecar. This featured a locking differential – enabling power to go to both the sidecar *and* the rear wheel when crossing rough ground. The Germans mounted machine guns in the sidecar and on the back of the bike, and Rommel used flying columns where pillion and sidecar passengers were gunners.

The British and Americans seldom used motorbikes like this, as instruments of attack. The British maintained their

Above, the weird and wonderful NSU HK101 Kettenkraftrad half-track probably first saw service with the Wehrmacht in the 1942 airborne invasion of Crete.

Right, the BMW R75 combo, a 750 cc 2-cylinder machine with locked differential drive to the sidecar, was the most famous German motorcycle of World War Two.

bikes for staff work; they also built some combinations along German lines (but less efficient), fitted with Vickers machine guns. They were more successful with their airfield defence bikes: BSA M20 bikes with a Bren gun and a sheet of armour plate along one side of the machine. When an airfield was strafed, the rider stopped his bike, laid it on its side, and took cover behind the armour plate, using his Bren as an anti-aircraft gun. Both the British and the Americans also built collapsible bikes which could be parachuted in cannisters – the Excelsior 'Welbike' parascooter was used by British troops, and the Cushman Motor Works in Nebraska supplied American airborne bikes.

Towards the end of World War Two, however, the motorcycle was gradually superseded as a military transport vehicle by the tougher and more adaptable Jeep, in the Allied Armies, and by the German 'Kubelwagen' on the other side.

The Biking Revolution

The postwar motorcycle combination but with a difference: a luxury model 998 cc British Vincent Series B Rapide harnessed to a German Steibe sidecar. The powerful V-twin made light work of even a loaded car. **Above right,** the Vincent engine.

Scooters were stylish in the 1960s but are no match for today's light motorcycles in performance terms. At present, only Vespa and Lambretta, both in Italy, still manufacture scooters, and sales are a fraction of what they were ten years ago.

After the Second World War, the British bike reigned supreme. British Nortons and Triumphs poured into America, in response to a demand created by the first appearance of a British bike at a major US motorcycle race – in 1949, at Daytona, Florida, when Dick Klamforth won on a 500 cc Manx Norton.

The dominance of the British firms concealed an overall, world-wide decline in motorbike sales and in biking generally. By the mid-1950s, Europe had not only recovered from the war: it was entering an age of affluence and rising living standards. For the first time, European workers could afford cars and European manufacturers, like Volkswagen, had developed cheap, reliable models of car to sell to them. As had happened twenty years earlier in America, bikers became a minority in Europe. Enthusiasts alone kept the motorcycle industry alive. Continental and British firms became sluggish and conservative: there weren't the profits around to spend on research, let alone racing (most European firms pulled out of racing in the late 1950s). Some development did go on, with the British branching out from 'singles' into 'twins', and the Germans concentrating on reliability – one-kick starting, foolproof electrics and shaft drive making the German bikes the nearest things to a car on two wheels. But it was development by default. Mechanics built the new British bikes, assembling and re-assembling the basic components in a back-street, workbench type of operation, fiddling a few more mph here and a little less vibration there. No one thought to re-design a bike from scratch, using modern methods, the methods of the engineer.

British ace, Geoff Duke, chasing McEwen in the 1951 Isle of Man TT race. Both men rode 500 cc Manx Nortons. The first TT was held in 1907 and was intended for production rather than racing machines. The first winner's average speed was under 40 mph. The famous 'mountain course' was introduced in 1911. British machines dominated 'the island' between the wars and in the immediate postwar period. Some of the glamour has rubbed off the TT in recent years as safer, custom-made tracks have been built elsewhere in Europe.

No one, that is, until the Japanese. When Honda first appeared with a team at the 1959 Isle of Man TT, people laughed. No one believed that these novices could build motorcycles. Within two seasons, Honda had swept every major race in Europe. The Japanese showed that they knew how to construct fast engines. They built from scratch for speed. In doing so, they ushered in the modern age of motorcycling, an age of precision machinery, as fine as a watch.

Though their racing triumphs made Japanese firms like Honda, Kawasaki, Suzuki and Yamaha into household names, they began by making and selling small bikes, almost mopeds – like the Honda 50 cc. With the 50s, they tapped a new market, of people who never thought of themselves as 'bikers'; people who had grown up with cars, but who were now ready for a cheaper and more manoeuvrable form of transport, often as a 'second vehicle'. Beginners soon learned how easy the 50s were to ride, with their automatic clutches. Gradually, as people got a taste for biking, they were ready to move up to a proper motorbike, a 125 or a 175, until, today, the 250 is probably the most common size on the road.

The Japanese had made motorbikes trendy. They caught the mood of the 1960s. Japanese bikes are light, sporty, easy to ride – and they perform! And Japanese manufacturers were not content to stay with the beginners' market. Inexorably, they moved up the sizes – 250s, 500s, 750s and above – wiping out the European makes on the way. None were more completely eclipsed than the British, whose firms have been closing down steadily since the war, until, now, there are two tiny companies, Scott and Silk.

Left, Rhodesian rider, Jim Redman, on a 350 cc Honda, powers towards victory in the 1964 Ulster Grand Prix. Modern road racing is a matter of highly-organised, factory sponsored teams, with a small band of professional riders travelling the world to win races. **Above**, the bike that began it all, the amazing Honda 50.

Road Racing

Road racing is the big-time of motorcycle sport. It has factory or sponsored teams, a season of Grand Prix racing around Europe, culminating in a World Championship in various classes, and a small international band of professional riders – men like Barry Sheene and Phil Read from Britain, Giacomo Agostini from Italy, Kenny Roberts from the USA and Teuvo Lansivouri from Finland.

In other words, road racing is just like motor car racing, except that it's a kind of poor relation, with less money involved, less publicity, and so on. As a sport, it's almost as old as motorcycling itself. As early as 1904, there was an International Motorcycle Cup Race in France. It lasted for three years (and was won by a Frenchman and two Austrians) before it broke up in confusion when all the leading nations protested against the rules; thus proving that good sportsmanship has never had much to do with international contests at any period.

The key skill in modern road racing is cornering. Riders heel their machines over at incredible angles and very high speeds. Look at a winning bike in the paddock after a race,

and you'll usually see the fairing scraped and torn where it's been rubbing along the ground! In effect, the shorter the 'line' you take through a corner, the more you need to lean over – and the faster you lap the course!

Though traditionally a European sport, it looks as if, in a few years' time, the United States will be the major road-racing country. American racing was, and still is, largely on dirt tracks, not roads. For many years, it was too far for Americans to come to race in Europe, and there still isn't enough cash in the sport to permit the jet-set, international lifestyles led by the top motor racing drivers, who fly all over the world from one race to the next. The first Anglo-American Race series was not held until 1971.

The most famous race in the motorbike racing calendar traditionally has been the Isle of Man TT. But the TT has

been the subject of intense controversy in recent years, and it's not included now in the Grand Prix circuit. Basically, the professionals feel that its hump-backed course, on ordinary roads without modern safety barriers, is simply too dangerous at modern speeds (laps of up to 100 mph). On the Continent, most Grand Prix races have moved on to specially constructed circuits like Spa in Belgium or Hockenheim in West Germany.

Above right, pictured in a Daytona 'Production' (or stock bikes) race are: No 24, Gary Fisher, on a BMW R90S; No 83, Steve McLaughlin, on a BMW R90S; No 31, Cook Neilson, on a 900 Ducati; and No 163, Reg Pridmore, on a BMW.

Left, Johnny Cecotto on a 750 cc Yamaha. Cecotto won Daytona, the US classic, in 1976. Note the split and cracked fairing, showing the way the bike has scraped along the ground to cut corners. Only centrifugal force keeps the rider 'upright'.

Right, the scene at the start of the Daytona 200 at Daytona Beach, Florida, USA. A combination of big prize money and being the first race meeting of the season makes Daytona a Mecca for top riders.

Left, French star, Phillipe Coulon, on his 750 cc Yamaha, tears into a Brands Hatch corner. Note the outstretched knee which acts as an air brake.

Above, sidecar aces, Werner Schwarzel (driver) and Andreas Huber, in their 680 Konig combi, racing at Brands Hatch make a formidable team.

Top-level road racing is a dangerous sport. Professionals manage to strike a balance between speed and safety but they will tell you that their emphasis is on safety; apart from anything else, an injury can keep them out of racing for several meetings, and cost them big money. But spills do happen, and to an outsider it's amazing how fast you can fall off a motorcycle and live – the unenviable record is currently held by Barry Sheene, who fell off at Daytona at 170 mph.

Competition Biking

Scrambling or motocross is cross-country running on motorbikes. It's probably the most popular kind of bike racing with riders and crowds alike. Rank amateurs can enjoy it as much as the superstars of the 'Continental Circus'; while, for the spectators, there are thrills, and mainly spills, galore. In fact, the only people who don't like it are the riders' wives and girlfriends, who have to spend their Sunday afternoons on freezing moorlands, miles from anywhere, watching their men get caked from head to foot in mud as they jump streams, slide down hillsides and generally attempt to tackle every natural obstacle there is.

Scrambling bikes have distinctive knobbly tyres and seem to spend most of their time flying through the air (politely known as 'jumping') when they're not lying flat on the ground with the rider underneath. Two-strokes have had great success in scrambling in recent years – these lighter engines can be mounted in lighter chassis, making for easier handling on rough ground. Scrambling and motocross are run under slightly different rules but are basically very similar sports and call for similar riding skills.

Scrambling has grown so big, with TV coverage and international meetings, that weekend riders who aren't so keen on speed and cut-throat competition have been turning to trials riding. Here you compete against yourself, and it's all down to handling skill. Trials riders ride against nature, with penalty points every time they stop or put a foot on the ground. The result is a bobbing, weaving symphony of skill, in which speeds may not go over fifteen mph. Trials bikes have the same knobbly tyres as scramblers, but they are small capacity (top weight would be about 250 cc).

Hill climbing is an even smaller sport than trials. It's very cheap, wholly amateur, and if you spend thirty minutes actually astride a bike in the season, you're doing badly, because the climbs are taking you too long. Elderly four-strokes can still climb a decent hill, and with the sun shining and other enthusiasts around you, it's a fun sport. It also appeals to impatient mountaineers.

Grass track is effectively speedway in the open air and on grass. Oval tracks are improvised by roping off a corner of a field. 'Grassers'' machines burn methanol and rely on engine braking to stop. Riders push them flat out down the straights and power-slide around the corners, speedway-style. As in speedway, the skill on grass is in riding flat out all the time. Top grassers sometimes turn pro with a speedway team but the career of a professional speedway rider isn't always glamorous and can be short, so not many grassers are tempted from their less dangerous sport.

Below, British ace Mick Andrews coaxes his 250 cc Yamaha through the 1975 6-day Scottish Trials to give him fourth place in the World Title positions.

Flying through the air (**right**) is daring young Heikki Mikkola from Finland on his Husqvarna in the 500 cc 1975 British Motocross Grand Prix.

Above, Robert Gross and passenger Andreas Graber came second in the 1975 European Sidecar Motocross Championship with their 750 cc Norton 'Wasp' combo.

They're off! **Left,** the start of the 1975 250 cc British Motocross Grand Prix shows expert action from (left to right) No 7 Hans Maisch (W. Germany on a Maico and No 5 Hakan Andersson (Sweden) riding a Yamaha; among others.

A Honda 400F works team scrambler with close-ratio transmission, chrome-moly steel frame and self-cleaning aluminium-alloy wheel rims.

Small Time Racers

So you want to race motorbikes? The thought of powering a 750 cc through a bend, while leaning your body over at an angle which constitutes a personal challenge to the laws of gravity, and at the same time fending off half a dozen grinning madmen doing the same thing an inch from your left shoulder doesn't horrify you as it should. In fact you'd like to spend all your time, money and energy doing just that; and you expect nothing in return. Very well. Most of the top professional road racers began in their teens at local or club level. Expert fathers, willing cousins or faithful friends are invaluable. Any kind of bike racing is 90 per cent preparation and recovery of your machine and 10 per cent actual riding. It's no wonder that so many stars come from biking families, where the father was a competitor himself.

Nowadays, every kind of racing – scrambling, grass track, speedway, hill climbs, trials or road racing – requires a specially built bike, as opposed to your regular street machine. Each sort of racing is a world to itself, so the first thing to decide is what sort you are interested in. It won't be easy to change later, although there are exceptions to this rule.

Ray and Pete are 'scramblers' who spend most of their leisure hours mastering the skills of cross-country biking. A car and a home-made trailer (**above**) for the special scrambler bikes are essential pieces of equipment – especially on the way home from races, when the bikes will be caked with mud. The bikes aren't suitable for road use.

Right, performing 'wheelies', or going uphill on one wheel, is a key scrambling skill. Scrambling or 'Motocross' (same sport, slightly different rules) is probably the most popular of all bike sports, open to beginners and virtual semi-professionals alike. Competition is fierce and a specially built machine – the boys ride Spanish Ossas – and plenty of practice are vital. Riders and machines must both be fit.

Left and below, Ray and Pete tackle a downhill run with mixed success. The rider is safe but the bike has its wheel bent and mudguard cracked in the headlong descent – meaning more hours of painstaking work in Ray's workshop (**right**).

Young hopefuls choose their field (often literally; a lot of bike racing goes on in fields), round up the money for a second-hand bike, join the relevant local club, and get on with it: for as long as they can afford the crippling cost of spares, maintenance, entrance fees, travel expenses, fuel, etc. Clubs for most sorts of bike racing are organised in national associations; or the motorbike magazines can give you the address of your nearest one.

The more successful you are in some ways, the harder it becomes. The top amateurs and semi-professionals in road racing – 'privateers' as they are called – have to compete with sponsored factory teams. Not only can the factories afford top riders and mechanics; often they won't even sell their most advanced machines to outsiders. Privateers lead a gypsy life, travelling in caravans round the 'Continental Circus' (the major European races) during the summer; working and saving all winter, spending nights tuning their bikes and days hoping they'll be good enough to be invited to join a factory team next year.

All types of motorbike racing are becoming more competitive and professional. Scrambling, or Motocross, used to be the amateur's favourite Sunday sport. But these days the true 'fun' riders are retreating into ever more obscure forms of mechanical torture, like trials or hill climbing.

Speedway!

Twenty-thousand fans gather round a floodlit track. The smell of the special methanol fuel hangs heavy in the night air. Four 500 cc JAP engines rev like mad, producing a shattering din. The tapes go up. The four riders blast down the straight and into the first turn at 50 mph, cornering in a shower of shale, the speedway ace's famous left boot jammed into the deck, the back wheel sliding and bucking across the cinders as if it had a life of its own.

That's speedway. It's a rough, tough sport that in many ways still seems to be a part of the jukebox era of the late 1940s and 1950s; even if today, it claims to be the second-biggest spectator sport in Britain, and the occasional race is screened on television.

Speedway isn't like any other motorbike sport. For a start, it's one hundred per cent professional. And it's the only sort of bike racing which appeals mainly to people who are not bikers themselves, who don't even own a motorbike. About as many speedway fans are bikers as greyhound racing fans keep greyhounds. Speedway is like greyhound racing in other ways, too. Both sports have the same slightly dated image. Both have their roots in the days before television, when people went out for their entertainment. And unlike soccer, neither has really managed to adapt to an era of mass communications.

A speedway bike is the nearest thing to a death trap on two wheels. One writer described them as 'delicate time bombs'. They have no gears and no brakes. In speedway, you ride flat out, getting round the oval track by literally manhandling the bike round the corners, sticking your steel-capped left boot in the dirt, letting the back wheel power-slide, while you wrench the front wheel almost at right angles to the rest of the bike. It's crazy, but it works. The result is seen in the speedway rider's characteristic stance, like a bow-legged cowboy with severe arthritis.

If you still can't see how they manage to keep control, the answer is that they often don't. Accidents abound. Speedway

aces tend to be small, quiet men with broken bones. They look like jockeys but live more like unsuccessful pop stars. They shuttle up and down the motorways in battered vans, eating at all-night cafes, playing one-night stands for not much money. Although everyone in speedway is professional, only a handful of top men make the big money.

Many speedway aces are Australians or New Zealanders (the latter have dominated the World Championship). The Scandinavian countries are also keen on the sport. The stars supplement their income during the summer season with grass track racing; and in the winter, with ice racing (for which the bikes have steel spikes stuck in their tyres) – this gives those who haven't broken anything all summer the chance to spend the winter in a nice, warm casualty ward!

Newcomers get into speedway either through succeeding at grass-tracking (mostly an amateur sport) and/or through open training sessions run by the speedway teams. The basic essentials are your own speedway bike and a steel boot. From then on, it all depends on how fast you can make those left-hand turns.

Russian ace, Alexander Sherbakov, racing on ice. Tyres are spiked (**see below**) for traction, making this sport, popular in Russia, Holland and Scandinavia, one for experts only!

Left, Jim McMillan, Bob Valentine and Terry Betts flog their Jawas round a bend in the World Team Cup Qualifying Round. England has dominated recent team events.

Below, the 500 cc Jawa, with its stripped to the bone look, is speedway's favourite bike.

Above, Ivan Mauger, New Zealand star and four times World Speedway champion, proves he is as brilliant on grass as he is on cinders.

The Motor Cycle as Science Fiction?

Above, American drag racing champion, T. C. Christiansen on his Dunstall-speed-equipped, twin-engined Norton, 'The Hogslayer'. Christiansen has since moved up to a three-engined bike.

European champion, John Hobbs, on 'The Hobbit'. The bike is powered by two supercharged Weslake 850 cc engines and does the quarter mile in the 8-second, 170 mph terminal speed brackets.

With drag bikes, we've reached the motorcycle as science fiction. Not 500 cc bikes, not 750 cc bikes, not 1000 cc bikes, but something like 3,500 cc! That's achieved with two, or even three, Harley Davidson engines in a single bike.

Drag racing with bikes: two riders racing one another from a standing start over the classic, straight, quarter-mile drag strip, clocking times in the eight-second bracket, and finishing at speeds of over 170 mph.

Drag racing began in the States, where it's a big professional sport now, and drag racing in Europe has a strongly American flavour to it. The sport grew out of the sort of contest featured in a succession of post-war Hollywood films, in which two 'juvenile delinquents' challenged each other to a 'chicken run' – an illegal trial of speed between two cars down a strip of deserted highway, with an admiring audience of supporters in attendance. One day some genius

Not so much a motorbike, more a mechanical miracle – Russ Collins' triple-engined Honda, 'the Acheson, Topeka and Santa Fé'. An eight-inch rear slick keeps it earthbound. World-class drag racing is now a competition between three or four men separated by sixteen hundredths of a second.

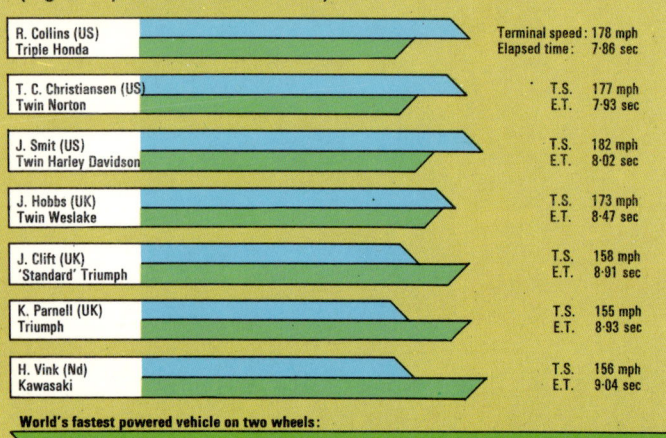

Drag Racing Speed Records
Below are the speeds set by the world's top drag racers – three Americans, the European champion and the fastest British riders. There are two sets of (unofficial) records: for terminal velocity (for first machine across the finishing line); and for elapsed time (highest speed over the distance).

R. Collins (US) Triple Honda	Terminal speed:	178 mph
	Elapsed time:	7·86 sec
T. C. Christiansen (US) Twin Norton	T.S.	177 mph
	E.T.	7·93 sec
J. Smit (US) Twin Harley Davidson	T.S.	182 mph
	E.T.	8·02 sec
J. Hobbs (UK) Twin Weslake	T.S.	173 mph
	E.T.	8·47 sec
J. Clift (UK) 'Standard' Triumph	T.S.	158 mph
	E.T.	8·91 sec
K. Parnell (UK) Triumph	T.S.	155 mph
	E.T.	8·93 sec
H. Vink (Nd) Kawasaki	T.S.	156 mph
	E.T.	9·04 sec

World's fastest powered vehicle on two wheels:
Don Vesco's 'Silver Bird' achieved 302·928 mph at Bonneville Salt Flats.

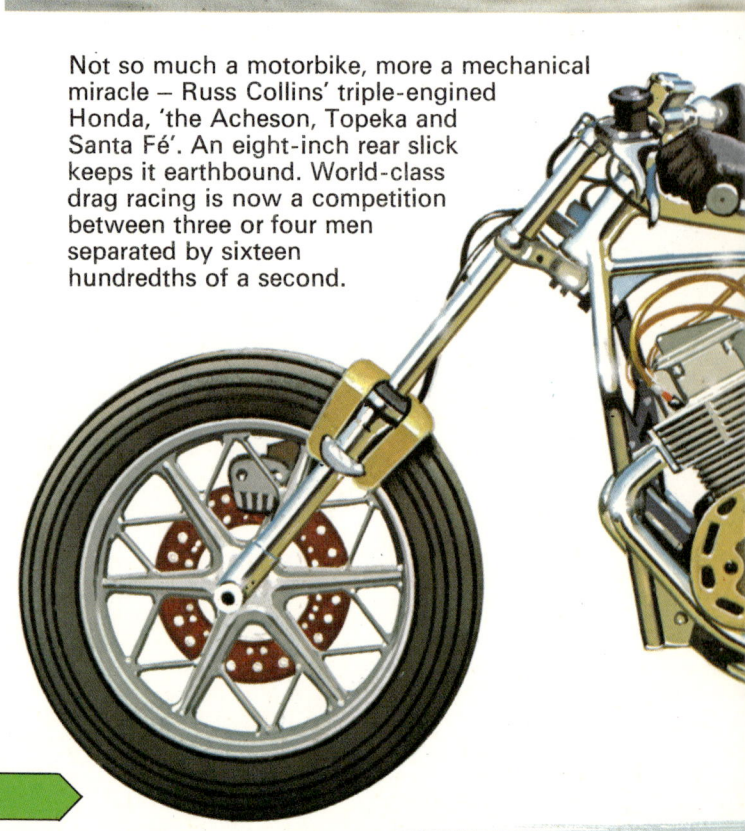

realised that the way to make his car go faster was to take the body off – the 'railer', or 'dragster', was born.

Naturally, anything a car owner can do, bikers reckon they can do better. Modern drag bikes really are engineering miracles; one feature of 'the motorcycle' – the ability to produce speed and acceleration over a short distance – has been taken out and bred to its ultimate pitch. Like any pure-bred beast, to some people the result is perfection; to others it's a monstrosity.

Drag racing can sound boring in cold print. In reality, it is one of the most incredible spectacles in motor sport: the ear-shattering noise, the smoking 'slicks' (special wide tyres used to ensure traction for the enormous engines), the sheer speed of the 'runs'.

Even in America, drag bikes are in the minority in drag racing, most of which is done in cars. In Britain, drag bikers form a minority of a minority. You can't buy a real drag bike: a nitro-burning, 'blown' (supercharged) nine-seconder – which would be a top competitor in British terms – has to be built from scratch by its rider. But any biker can get into drag by joining a club, buying a second-hand machine (it won't be a nitro-burning, nine-seconder!) and working his way up through the classes, gaining knowledge en route.

Perhaps because they are such a minority, drag racers are a friendly bunch who welcome newcomers to the sport. They form a distinct group from other bikers, except for chopper owners, with whom they have a lot in common. They are close, too, to the essentially American world of custom cars – rebuilding and repainting cars into extraordinary, fantasy vehicles. There is a definite bond in Europe between custom car owners, chopper freaks and drag bikers: from Lyons to Huddersfield, all of them are dreaming the American dream.

Left, fastest man on two wheels – Don Vesco in his special 'Silver Bird' streamliner, achieved 302.928 mph at Bonneville Salt Flats on 28 September 1975 in the twin-engined Yamaha.

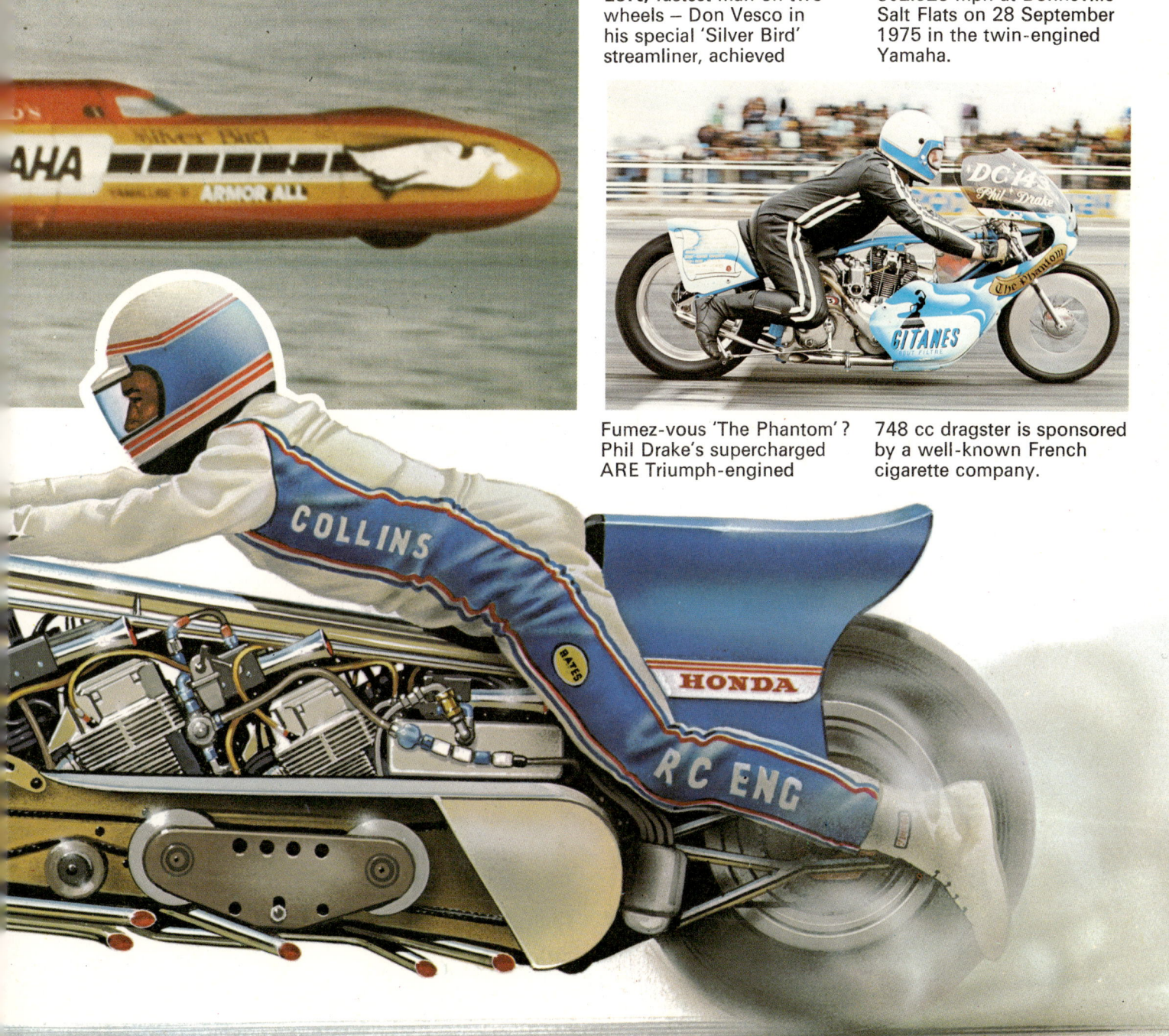

Fumez-vous 'The Phantom'? Phil Drake's supercharged ARE Triumph-engined 748 cc dragster is sponsored by a well-known French cigarette company.

Lightweight Bikes

Small bikes are ridden by all kinds of people: learners, students, midwives, friendly neighbourhood policemen and every French and Italian beach bum under 30!

Small bikes led the resurgence of biking in the late 1950s and early 1960s, after its eclipse by the car. In America, traditionally a big bike market, sales of small bikes began to pick up noticeably in the late 1950s. In Europe, the scooter craze, spearheaded by the Vespa, which had appeared as early as 1946, showed those who had eyes to see that interest in two-wheelers went beyond a few hard-core enthusiast-mechanics and social outlaws. The scooter was, and is, unstable and performs poorly compared with a light motorbike. But it made motorcycling look like fun.

The European manufacturers, notably the British, couldn't see it. It was left to the Japanese, with the famous Honda

The Carabella Marquesa 175 MX.

The Hodaka 100 Trial 'Road Toad' – not really a trials bike but typical of the sort of bikes currently used for trials.

50 cc in the vanguard, to produce successful small bikes and tap a vast new market of first-time bikers. You can ride a small bike straight away; it uses little fuel, so it's cheap; and its manoeuvrability makes it ideal for city riding.

'You meet the nicest people on a Honda' was one of the early small bike advertising slogans. And these bikes did introduce a whole new class of people to biking – women. Girls who thought twice about jumping on to a 500 cc Norton, were happy to ride the easy, automatic step-through Honda 50.

From the 50 ccs, the Japanese moved up to the 125s, 175s, 250s, with equal success. 'The Japanese were passionless about making motorcycles,' an American writer reported; and he was right. Their bikes are tailored to meet the demands of the mass market in the same way as transistor radios or televisions.

Then there are the mini-bikes. First produced as weapons – they were dropped in cannisters to paratroopers in World War Two – they have become a civilian gimmick. No Grand Prix team is complete without a clutch of 'monkey bikes' for working around the paddock.

Left, two 123 cc Suzukis: the RV-125 Tracker (left) and the TS-125 Duster.

Monkey bikes are fun, as the 70 cc Dax Honda (right) proves. But they began as wartime necessities.

Casal 50 Trial – from Portugal – in the currently fashionable semi-scrambler, on/off road style.

Like most German (and Swedish) bikes, the Zündapp 125 is almost too well-built of top-quality components.

Left, Motobecané 125 Electronique from the last French manufacturer.

Below, the 50 cc Kreidler RS Florett from the Dutch Van Veen Company.

Mainstream Bikes

250s are perfect for town. What's more, learners can ride them. There are probably more 250s than anything else on the road, but real bikers find them too light for long runs. In the mind of Mr Average, there's an idea that the bigger and more powerful a bike is, the more dangerous it is to ride. Not so, say most bikers: they feel safer on the larger machines. Take a 250 from London to Edinburgh and you'll begin to realise why they feel this way. Crosswinds and overtaking vehicles affect the bike's stability. The bike doesn't have the power to get you out of trouble while, from the point of view

This weird looker is the Swedish Hagglunds XM74, a 345 cc bike which began life as a military machine. Note shaft drive and 8-spoke wheels.

of comfortable and speedy progress, you'll find it hard to maintain a motorway speed without taxing the engine, especially if you've got gear or a pillion passenger aboard.

All of which begins to make the case for the bigger bikes clearer – 500 ccs and up. 500s are the classic size for road-racing bikes. The Japanese consolidated their hold over the modern market when they brought out their 500s in the late 1960s. They introduced each new model *at its fastest*, then spent the next couple of years making it go slower. Traditional European practice was to introduce a new model at its

Italian styling combines with a V-twin, 4-stroke engine to give the sporty Motor/ Morini 350 a top speed of around 100 mph.

Right, the BMW 75, a 750 cc flat-twin has the refinements of top electrics, shaft drive and high-speed cruising comfort.

Unfortunately still only a design concept, the prototype Norton 76 (**below**), is perhaps the last example of a long and glorious history of British superbikes. Capable of

120 mph and up to *50 mpg at a low retail price*, the bike was designed, refined and built by the twelve survivors of the Norton Villiers company in Wolverhampton.

The Bultaco 370, latest from this leading Spanish manufacturer, whose bikes have been particularly successful in trials, with a substantial off-road range.

Like all Japanese machines, the Honda CB400F scores on combining modern, lightweight engineering with racing performance: a four-cylinder, air-cooled, four-stroke.

slowest and then improve its performance over the ensuing few years on the market.

The Japanese were quick, too, about tailoring their machines to European – and particularly American – ideas of good design. The early Japanese bikes were ugly beasts to Western eyes, with pressed-steel frames, square headlights and leading-linked front forks. Their punch was in the power pack: just as the Honda 50s performed on a par with the 125 cc machines of the 1950s, so the bigger Hondas compared with existing bikes twice their size. Honda rethought

the design of their new bikes, kept the engines and produced the Honda Hawk (250 cc) and Super Hawk (305 cc), with tubular frames, round headlights, telescopic front forks and the look of modern biking. The Super Hawk did over 100 mph, and incorporated the 'luxuries' the Germans had introduced to motorcycling, like reliable electrics, including an electric starter. The Super Hawk, a vertical twin with single overhead camshaft, swept the US market, in its design, performance and its wide appeal to bikers and non-bikers alike, a worthy predecessor to today's 'super-bikes' . . .

Above, the Italian 6-cylinder Benelli 750 SE1 and **(below),** the Soviet 650 cc Cossack Ural combination.

Superbikes

With the 750 cc class, and with their even larger and more powerful successors – the 'superbikes' – we're talking about bikes for bikers once again. This is the world of the enthusiast; and every enthusiast has his favourite make or model which he'll defend to the death against every other make or model. As a result, it's in this big, sports bike range that the European manufacturers, plus Harley Davidson, have staged their last stand against the all-conquering Japanese manufacturers. (There are also competitive European and US makes in racing bikes – like the Czech CZ in motocross.)

The challenge to the Japanese has worked, up to a point. The Italian Laverda or Ducati, the MV Agusta, the German BMWs, the British Norton Commando, all have their partisans. But the Commando, with what is basically a 1950s engine, has no electric starter and suffers from that curse of British bikes – oil leakage; while Triumph, faced with designing a new engine, settled instead for an inspired piece of tinkering.

The Japanese-made 750s also had their problems when they first came out. To this date, they are struggling to get the handling right, but they scored with a sophistication new to most bikers – a variety of cylinder arrangements, rev counters, disc brakes, electric starters.

In the early 1970s, bikes began a steady climb in power and performance which continues to the present. This resulted in machines like the Kawasaki 903 cc Z1, the first double-overhead-camshaft, four-cylinder, mass-production bike, with a 120 mph cruising speed and an ability to travel a quarter of a mile in 12.5 seconds from a standing start.

The Suzuki RE5 749 cc machine is one of the few bikes to adopt the rotary 'Wankel' engine for mass production purposes. The power-plant is water cooled.

1. Kawasaki 900 cc (Japan)
2. BMW 900 cc (Germany)
3. MV Agusta 750 cc (Italy)
4. Moto Guzzi 750S (Italy)
5. Laverda 980 cc (Italy)

Right, a Ducati 860GT V-twin has distinctive, chunky lines and a double 'open cradle' frame, originally designed for racing bikes at Imola.

Far right, a British Silk 700S with a dummy petrol tank to improve balance (the real tank is the triangle below the false one). The Silk is virtually the only British motorcycle in independent production.

DUCATI
860

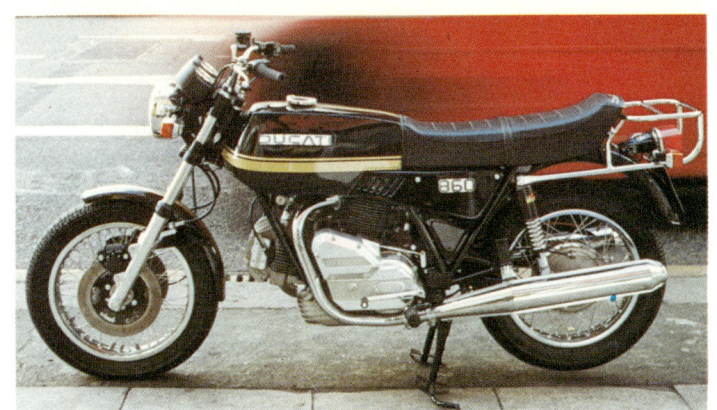

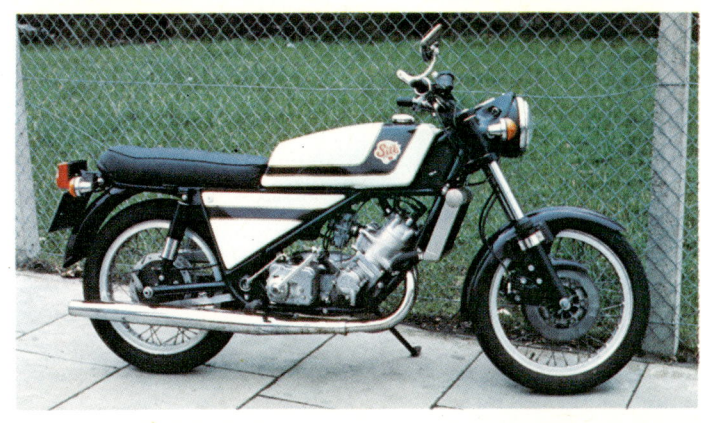

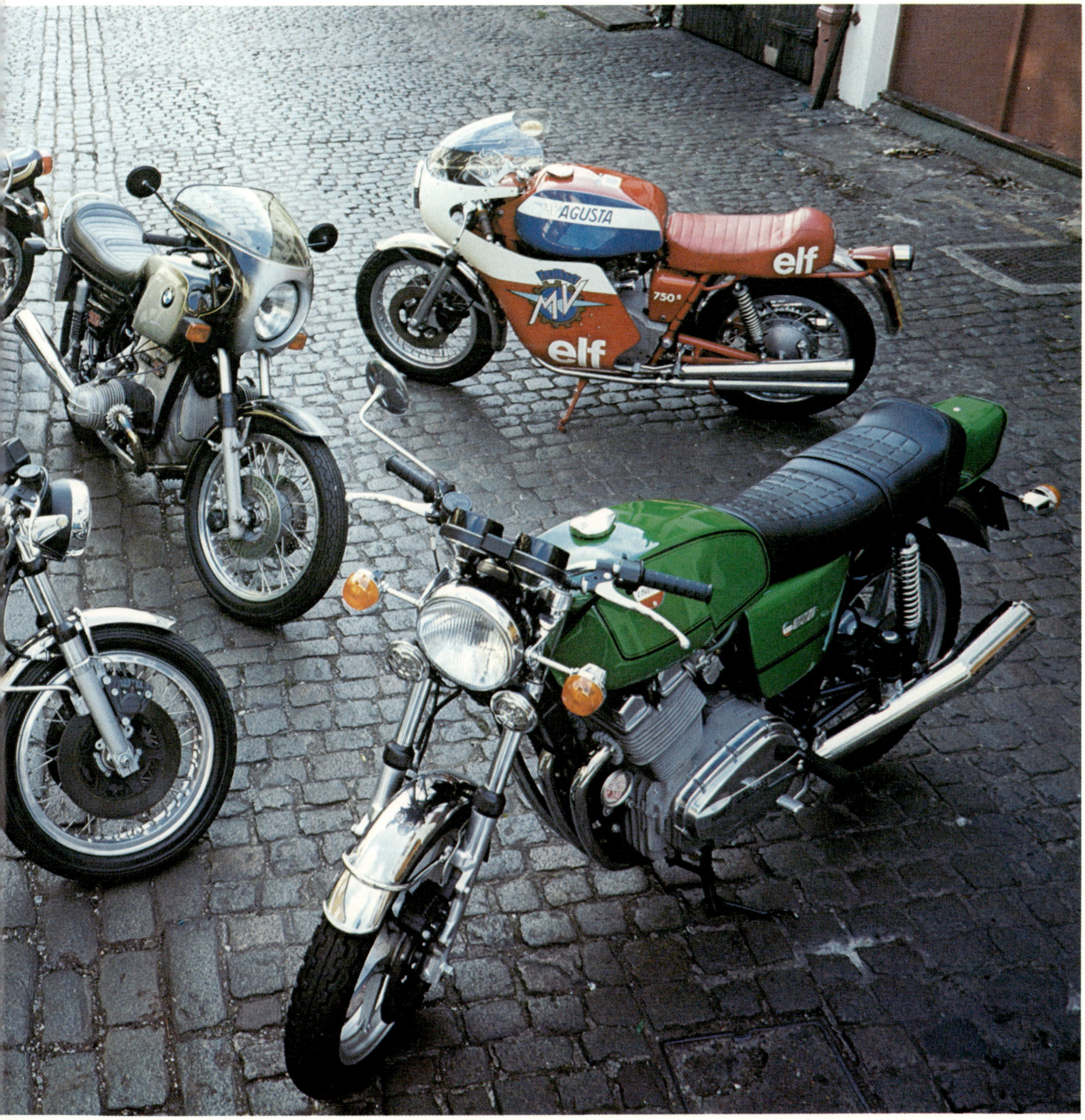
AGUSTA
elf
750 S
elf

Heavyweight Cruisers

For all their impressive performance, 'superbikes' are simply big motorcycles. The difference between a Kawasaki 903 cc and a Honda 250 cc is pretty much 653 cc! The 'giants' of the motorcycling world are completely different animals. Perhaps four or five models in the world qualify for the title of 'giant'; and they don't do it on speed or performance alone. On the contrary, the giants are mostly sluggish and unimpressive performers for their size. Their appeal remains a mystery to most bikers. You have to be a special sort of person to ride a giant. The Harley, the Munch Mammoth, the Moto Guzzi, the Van Veen – these are the true giants; luxury touring bikes; monsters which can carry a rider, a passenger, tents, suitcases, sleeping bags and a staff of domestic servants (well, 60-70 kilograms of luggage at any rate) with the unconcerned ease of an elephant carrying a howdah.

Giants are the machines to ride on the German autobahns, the British motorways, the long straight roads of central France, the Italian autostradas, sweeping in graceful curves hundreds of metres above the Mediterranean; or to take on the American Interstates, rolling out the miles and days through Kansas cornfields, where there is nothing but dust and heat and small-town diners, a hundred miles apart. With their full windscreens, excess of chrome, crash bars, enormous weight and non-return throttles, giants not only look great, they are the most comfortable way to motorcycle all day at cruising speeds in the 80 mphs. You can even take your hands off the handlebars to roll a cigarette or study the map.

The Moto Guzzi V1000 matches peak power with easy riding thanks to automatic transmission, a combination stand/handbrake and linked front and rear brakes.

Left, the Munch Mammoth 4 1200 TTS began as a typical German attempt to marry a car engine and a motorbike frame. The current vertical-four engine derives from the NSU cars.

Right, the Honda GL-1000 Gold Wing, like the other aristocrats of modern biking, solves the overheating problems of its horizontal, 4-cylinder engine by being water-cooled.

Lower left, the Dutch Van Veen OCR-100 has a 996 cc rotary engine, water-cooled, with 4-speed gear box, shaft drive, magnesium alloy wheels and disc brakes front and rear.

maxidyne

Perhaps the most famous of all big bikes, the Harley Davidson FLH-1200 'Electra Glide', has hardly changed its design, with the classic V-twin engine, in 15 years. Automatic ignition has replaced the kick start but the 'buddy seat' style saddle and abundance of showy chrome are unmistakably Harley!

Café Racers

The time: the early 1960s. The place: a motorway café, fifteen miles north of London, England. The tea is hot and strong, the windows are steamed over, the giant American juke box in the corner flashes constantly. A group of sullen-looking youths in black leather jackets and oil-stained jeans is scattered about the rickety tables, most of its members looking bored. One of them raises his head and says:

'Let's go for a burn-up.'

Everybody jumps up and the speaker goes over to the juke box and puts on the Shangri-Las' 'Leader of the Pack'. As the first chords belt out, the youths grab their heavy gloves off the tables and pile into the car park outside. A row of big, gleaming bikes, 350s and upwards, stand, tuned and polished to perfection. The youths jump on their machines. The bark of kick starters is followed by the throaty roar of well-kept engines. And they're off; wheeling out onto the highway; 60 ... 70 ... 80 ... 100 miles an hour; down to a nearby roundabout, around it once, and back up and inside the door of the café before the record has stopped playing.

That was café racing. The youths were called 'rockers' and the image they created – of the black, leather-clad outlaw – has stuck with motorcycling ever since (reinforced by the even more extreme, anti-social image of the American Hell's Angels). The rockers' bikes were the first café racers. The point of a cafe racer is to make an ordinary production bike into the closest possible approximation of a racing machine. You do this by adding a whole range of goodies to it – the most familiar being the distinctive racing 'fairings' (moulded bodywork to lessen wind resistance); and the pocket-sized 'clip-ons' (racing handlebars). There are also special chrome brackets to set out the headlights; moulded fibreglass petrol tanks with quick-release caps; moulded tank and seat units which alter your body position to a racing crouch; rear-set foot rests (which do the same); racing tyres; 'ally' (magnesium alloy) wheels; 'gaiters' for the suspension (rubber telescoping); straight-through exhaust pipes with some baffles removed to give a deeper, throatier engine sound; different exhaust arrangements, like 'Siamese pipes' or 'four-in-one'; chromed or – the current fashion – blackened exhausts; bell mouths on the carburettors; and more.

Like most fashions, café racing filtered down from the few to the many, becoming diluted on the way. These days, you don't have to be a rocker to own a café racer bike. You don't even have to do it yourself – you can buy most of the 'parts' from specialist firms. You can see people dressing 125s and 250s as café racers, whereas rockers would have turned up their noses (or, more likely, their boots and fists) at anything under a 350 cc. Although so much inspired by the American way of life, the café racing craze is only now hitting America.

As a café racer, all you really need is self-love. Café racing is about your image of yourself, as reflected in your bike. Just as some people are pop stars in the privacy of their bathrooms, so many a biker is a secret café racer at heart.

Right, this Kawasaki 1100 in a Dunstall conversion, belongs to the leader of the British pop group, Emerson, Lake and Palmer. **Below left,** in the background, the production Kawasaki 900Z1; in front, would you believe, it's the same bike? This is the Dunstall variant. **Below,** inside the workshops of Dunstall's, a leading designer of ready-made café racers. Customising parts for the Kawasaki skeleton are (clockwise from rear), fitted seat unit and tank cover, fairing and windscreen, front mudguard, magnesium alloy wheels and (between) exhaust mufflers and clip-ons. 4–into–2 exhaust pipes, foot rest and gear change are behind.

Above, two examples of the John Player Special 'replica' Norton Commando. Based loosely on the Team Norton machines, these are regarded by many enthusiasts as the ultimate 'caff' racer. **Below,** the 'Gus Kuhn' Commando Special features enlarged aluminium petrol tank.

Choppers

Choppers are the freak's café racers. Like café racers, they are altered or customised motorbikes. But just how altered can you get before the thing ceases to be a bike at all, and becomes an object to park outside your 'pad' and invite your fellow freaks to come and look at and discuss in such critical terms as 'Wow, man' and 'Far out'?

The answer to this question is what divides chopper owners from their fellow bikers. Many bikers see choppers as deformed motorcycles, spectacular to look at, but awkward and uncomfortable to ride. Chopper owners, on the other hand, think that they've invented the motorcycle as an object of beauty. To them, an altered front end is pure poetry. In America, in particular, chopper freaks have displayed a

wealth of creative mechanical ingenuity and imagination.

'Choppers' first appeared in America in the 1950s, when a production Harley Davidson weighed around 320 kilograms. The simplest way to make it go faster was to take all the junk off – to 'chop' it. Nowadays, a chopper means any bike with an altered or extended front end. Obviously it's a much bigger job to build a chopper than a café racer – you're reconstructing the bike rather than adding optional extras. It also involves having a different image of yourself. Choppers go with long hair and psychadelic rock; café racers with leathers and toughness. Put another way, it's the age-old division between poet and philosopher, and sportsman and warrior.

Choppers belong to America. They only became fashionable in Europe with the film, *Easy Rider* (1968). European police and traffic regulations are a lot less amenable to funny-looking motorbikes than they are in America (and here, the hostility towards bikers caused by the original café racers

42

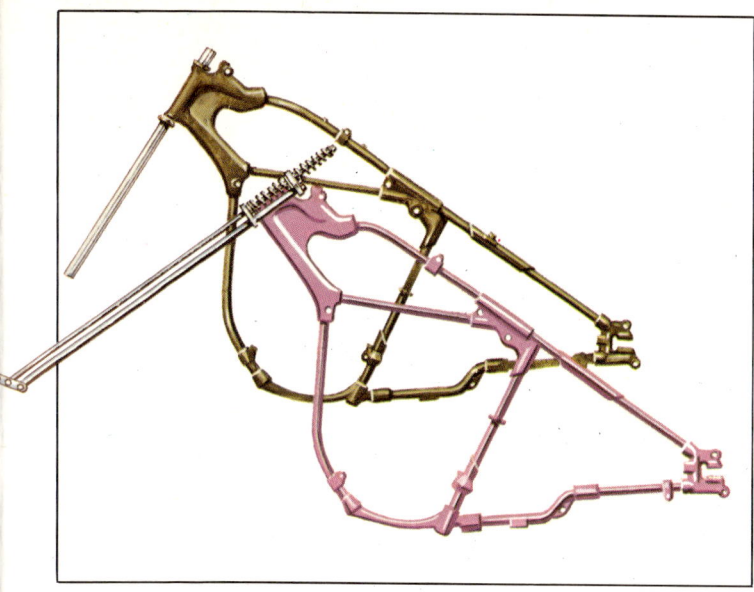

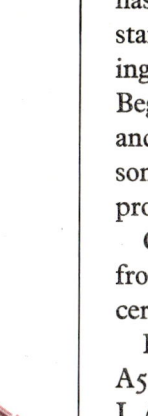

has lingered to affect the chopper owners). European living standards are still far enough behind America to make building a chopper an expensive business, for enthusiasts only. Beginners tend to build choppers with very long extensions and lots of rake (on the front forks), which is why you see some choppers wobble from a standing start. Too much rake produces excess 'trail', affecting the bike's steering.

Choppers are not built for speed. They certainly get you from one place to another but the chopper rider's main concern is how he, and his machine, look while getting there.

Besides, riding your chopper in the pouring rain down the A58½ just isn't the same as wheeling from San Francisco to L.A. at ten o'clock at night with your shirt off and the warm California air around you. Travelling is part of the American Dream, and on a chopper you have time to dream, to imagine yourself the hero of 'The Ballad of Easy Rider'. It's hard to be an easy rider in Europe.

Above, a classic 'rake' job (increasing the angle of the front forks) on a Harley frame. Chopper freaks prefer old-style, rigid-suspension frames because they set seat and rear mudguard as low over wheel as possible. **Below** is a completed trike, part drag-car, part chopper.

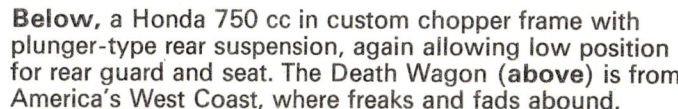

Below, a Honda 750 cc in custom chopper frame with plunger-type rear suspension, again allowing low position for rear guard and seat. The Death Wagon (**above**) is from America's West Coast, where freaks and fads abound.

Owners and Riders

Flo takes on the London traffic on her stalwart little Puch . . .

Malcolm Clube, biker extraordinary, with his collection : (left to right) JAP grass tracker, Triton and MV Agusta.

Malcolm Clube is a motorcycle enthusiast and amateur racing driver:

I've had about a hundred and fifty bikes in my time. At the moment I've got two Honda 50s, a 7R AJS, a Manx Norton, a 750 cc Triton Road Racer, a 500 cc CStar JAP, a 1916 Royal Enfield and, the pride of my collection, an MV Agusta 750. I used to road race, then I did some grass tracking, but now I own a racing car. I don't ride the bikes much in town except the Hondas, because there are so many mugs on the road. I ride the MV regularly on long runs – just take off and ride around Europe for a couple of days, and back. Stop for a coffee and move on. You've got to shift to do 600 miles in a day. I don't like clubs – they're terribly *slow*. They want to stop and drink and talk instead of riding. I like to go far and fast. My MV really looks the business: I bought it because it has tremendous charisma. I keep it mint. It takes me half a day to clean it after a good run. The police stop me a bit, usually just to look at it. Police motorcyclists are often enthusiasts too. I use my head about speed, and keep a lookout for the law all the time, which takes some doing when you're checking the road, other traffic, everything at 100 mph. You know something? I don't give a damn about my racing car really, or any car. I only care about the MV.

Flo Fothergill, art student, riding her first motorbike:
I bought a Puch Maxi S when I started at art college and I use it mainly for commuting between home and college – that's about half an hour's ride. After half an hour, I get too cold. It's tremendous fun to ride because you go straight through all the traffic jams. When I first rode it, I was terrified: if you're used to driving a car and being surrounded by thick metal, you feel very vulnerable. No one taught me to ride. They sold me a helmet and fitted a mirror and off I went, very precariously. At least, having driven a car, I knew what a menace motorcyclists can be, so I didn't whizz up the middle of the road all the time. As a girl, I know I look awful riding in the winter, but in the summer you can buzz around in a T-shirt and there's a French look about it.

My bike is 49 cc and it has pedals, which is an advantage when I run out of petrol. The petrol tank is badly designed: you can't see in it and it has no gauge. You get very adept at listening for the pop-pop sound and changing to the reserve tank with your foot. I've had quite a lot of trouble with the bike, but I think I got a bad one. The first time I brought it back to the garage was because every time I switched the headlights on, the hooter went! The other thing is, it only has a 35 mph top speed, but I'm not sure I'd be safe on anything faster. Of course, I'm lucky, because I have access to other people's cars as well.

Flo Fothergill

Doug Brand's burly frame makes his Triumph 'Saint', police pursuit bike look like a moped.

Doug Brand is a police motorcyclist in London:

All of us in traffic division double as motorcyclists and car drivers, and I personally agree with people who say that, if you learn to ride a motorcycle before you learn to drive, you'll be a better driver. Motorcyclists learn to notice road surfaces and conditions, and this is very valuable, especially when we drive police cars at high speed. We get two lots of tuition, an initial and an advanced course. By the end of the three weeks' initial training, they start to teach you to stand up on the footrest, grip the tank with your knees and put your arms out. It's frightening for a novice but it teaches you very quickly what a bike will do. Then, when you go out on patrol in central London, you soon find that drivers these days are looking for other cars: they really don't see motorcyclists. It's a case of having to learn the basic skills of town riding to survive!

We deal mainly with traffic flow and accidents. I don't believe motorcyclists are more dangerous than other road users: most of them are more skilful, in fact. The danger comes from the young riders. There's no proper training for motorcyclists in Britain, and young lads tend to ride the modern light bikes the same way they would ride a pedal bike. The way most bikers improve is, they join a club and people laugh at them, so they calm down and start riding properly. We see motorcyclists in accidents that wouldn't injure a car driver, and they tend to get very complicated injuries of the thighs and the pelvis. And in summer, youngsters often ride without proper protective clothing. The police wear heavy clothing all year, which is uncomfortable, but we know that if you come off, you're likely to slide, and we see the results of sliding on skin all too often.